This Pokémon Annual belongs to:

....

Age: ....

My Pokémon buddy is:

....

EGMONT
We bring stories to life

First published in Great Britain in 2018
by Egmont UK Limited
The Yellow Building, 1 Nicholas Road, London W11 4AN

ISBN 978 1 4052 9117 0
68609/002
Printed in Italy

Parental guidance is advised for all craft and colouring activities. Always ask an adult to help when
using glue, paint and scissors. Wear protective clothing and cover surfaces to avoid staining.

Stay safe online. Egmont is not responsible for content hosted by third parties.

Written and designed by Cloud King Creative.
With special thanks to Bird Keeper Toby for his expertise and help throughout.

Egmont takes its responsibility to the planet and its inhabitants very seriously.
We aim to use papers from well-managed forests run by responsible suppliers.

POKéMON

ANNUAL 2019

CONTENTS

GREETINGS FROM ALOLA!

Join Ash Ketchum and his buddy, Pikachu, as they continue their Alolan adventures!

There's plenty to explore on the tropical islands, with exciting new Pokémon to discover and interesting people to learn from along the way – including expert Trainers Kiawe, Lana, Mallow, Sophocles and Lillie.

Team Rocket have arrived in the Alola region and are ready to swipe Ash's prized Pokémon at every turn. Can Ash outsmart them and continue his quest to become a Pokémon Master?

Turn the page to join Ash on his journey – read new stories, try the puzzles and meet rare Pokémon and Ultra Beasts to discover which creatures could help you in your next battle.

ASH IS BACK!

Ash felt at home in the Alola region ever since he arrived there on vacation. He enrolled in the Pokémon School in Alola to continue his training to become a Pokémon Master. The Islands have so many strange and exciting Pokémon still to be revealed!

Pikachu's tail is shaped like a lightning bolt.

These red pouches are used to store electricity.

ASH KETCHUM

10-year-old Ash is from Pallet Town in the Kanto region. His travels far and wide have rewarded him with new friends, and the discovery of hundreds of different Pokémon. Ash is always keen to learn more and test himself, and knows he must complete the island challenge on each of Alola's major islands if he is to become an even stronger Trainer.

Learn more about Pikachu's moves on page 68.

PIKACHU

Pikachu has travelled with Ash as his Pokémon partner since Ash's early days as a Trainer. He may look cute and friendly, but this Electric-type Pokémon is not afraid to battle against any creature, big or small. His electric moves are a sight to behold!

Cool **KIAWE** rides a Charizard to school, passed down to him from his grandfather. Together, they deliver milk from the family's farm. Kiawe wears a Z-Ring given to him by Kahuna Olivia of Akala Island.

A quiet and shy girl at school, **LANA** is more relaxed at home with her family. Mallow looks out for Lana in class and is more like a big sister to her than a friend. Lana is interested in Water-type Pokémon.

Energetic **MALLOW** never gives up once she starts a project. She lives with her father and brother and their home is also the local restaurant. Mallow loves helping out with the cooking there.

Kind and polite, **LILLIE** loves studying different Pokémon and even sounds like a Pokédex when talking about them! She was scared of touching Pokémon until she caught her own Alolan Vulpix.

SOPHOCLES loves anything electrical. He's curious about how the Rotom Pokédex works and has even taken one apart to see what makes it tick. His favourite Pokémon are Electric-types.

ROCKET RIVALS

It was only a matter of time before Team Rocket caught up with Ash, as they follow his every move. Now Jessie, James and Meowth have landed in the Alola region and are ready to use every dirty trick they know to capture Pikachu and the other rare Pokémon that live there.

JAMES

He may appear hard on the outside, but James has a soft spot for each of his Pokémon, forming a strong bond with those who travel with Team Rocket. Pokémon are the only real friends that James has ever had.

MEOWTH

Meowth is the third member of the terrible trio that makes up Team Rocket and has travelled far and wide with Jessie and James. Unlike other Pokémon, Meowth has a unique skill – he has taught himself to speak!

JESSIE

Jessie is the toughest member of Team Rocket, which is why she made herself team leader. She's vain, has a short temper and does not always treat her own Pokémon well.

Help Team Rocket find the Pokémon they need to take on Ash and Pikachu.

START

Mareanie

Bewear

Mimikyu

MIMIKYU ☐
BEWEAR ☐
MAREANIE ☐
WOBBUFFET ☐

Wobbuffet

FINISH

THE ANSWERS ARE ON PAGE 69.

11

PERFECT POKÉ BALLS

Grab your pens, then finish colouring each square to produce some perfect Poké Balls, ready for your next catch.

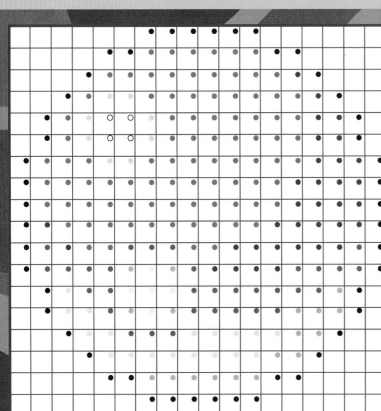

POKÉ BALL

This is the standard Poké Ball used for catching Pokémon.

GREAT BALL

The Great Ball has a higher rate of success in catching Pokémon than the Poké Ball.

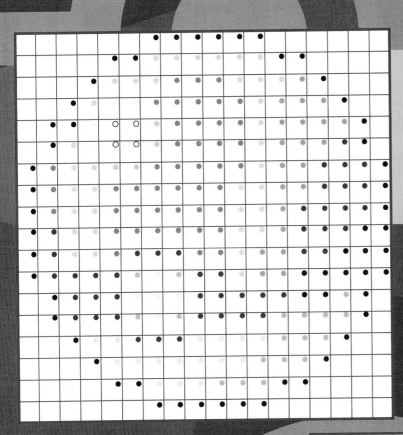

HYPER BALL

The Hyper Ball has a higher rate of success in catching Pokémon than the Great Ball.

DUSK BALL

The Dusk Ball is useful for catching Pokémon at night and in caves.

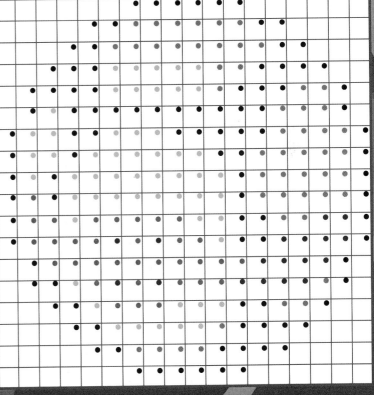

HIT THE BEACH

Today's Pokémon hunt is taking place on the beach!
Circle 10 Poison- and Water-type Pokémon lurking in the scene.

Which poisonous Pokémon did you find?
Unscramble the letters in its name. *I M A N E A R E*

THE ANSWERS ARE ON PAGE 69.

SUDOKU

Draw pictures in the grids so that each column and each row contains ONLY ONE of each symbol.

Difficulty level: **EASY**

Difficulty level: **TOUGH**

Difficulty level: **SUPER TOUGH**

THE ANSWERS ARE ON PAGE 69.

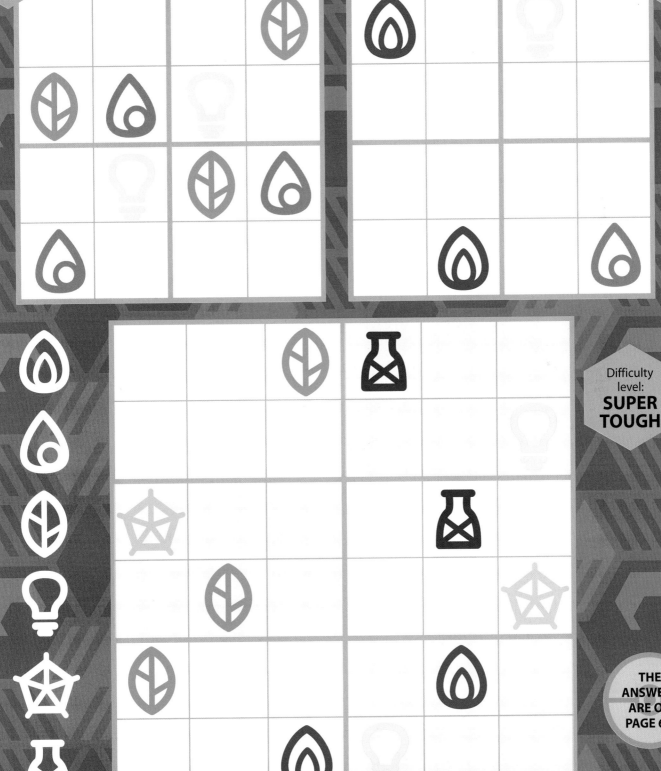

A DREAM ENCOUNTER

Drrring! It was 7.30 in the morning, but Ash was still fast asleep in bed.

"Come on, Ash. Get up!" said Rotom Dex, turning off the alarm. "You've breakfast to eat and your face to wash before school."

He floated over to a sleepy Pikachu and said, "You need to wake up too, Pikachu!"

Ash began to murmur. "I understand, Solgaleo! I promise, Lunala!"

"He's talking in his sleep," sighed Rotom. "Litten, you're up!"

With a quick leap and flick of its tail, Litten managed to wake its Trainer, at last!

"Aw, man …" Ash complained, rubbing his eyes. "You could have found a nicer way to wake me up!"

"We did try!" Rotom replied.

Ash began to get dressed. "I can't stop thinking about the most incredible dream I had … least, I think I did," he said.

But there was no time for Ash to explain. He had exactly five minutes to eat his breakfast and head out of the door.

On the way to school, Pikachu raced ahead into the bushes.

"Hey, Pikachu! Wait up!" Ash called.

"What has Pikachu found?" Rotom wondered.

Ash walked towards Pikachu to take a closer look at what his buddy had discovered.

"A **Pokémon**? Hmm … it's still asleep," he said, carefully picking up the creature. It looked friendly enough.

Ash stared down at the purple Pokémon and suddenly remembered. "My dream! I made a promise … that I'd find you!"

Rotom was confused. "You made a promise? When? Where? Who did you promise?" he said.

But Ash didn't answer. "I wonder what kind of Pokémon it is …" he said instead.

"Leave it to me," bleeped Rotom, searching his database. "Hmm, that's unusual! My research doesn't contain any Pokémon data for it at all!"

At the Pokémon School, everyone had arrived for the day's lessons. Everyone except Ash. Professor Kukui was worried – Ash had left the house before him, he should have arrived at school by now.

"He's probably trying to catch a Pokémon somewhere," Sophocles suggested.

Seconds later, Ash appeared.

"Professor Kukui!" Ash panted. "It was the one I saw in a dream last night! I made a promise to somebody that I'd find it and take care of it, and then, hmph … why do people always forget their dreams?" he cried.

"We've discovered a Pokémon that's not in my database!" Rotom explained.

"OK, Ash, calm down and tell me more about this Pokémon," Professor Kukui replied. "Where is it now?"

"Right here, in my bag," Ash said. He hurriedly unzipped his backpack to reveal a cute-looking Pokémon, snuggled next to Rowlet.

Everyone stood back in amazement, as the Pokémon floated into the air.

"Wow! We need to investigate this Pokémon!" said Professor Kukui excitedly. He just loved researching new creatures.

"It's giggling! How cute!" smiled Lillie. "Hmm … let's call it 'Nebula' … no, 'Nebby'!"

"Why 'Nebby'?" asked Ash.

"It has stars glittering inside it. And see how it floats like a cloud? Well, since a nebula is a cloud of gas with stars inside …" Lillie told the others.

"**Nebby**!" Ash agreed. "Great name!"

"Then it's decided," smiled Professor Kukui.

Suddenly, though, Nebby let out a piercing scream. Everyone covered their ears, as tears streamed from the creature's eyes.

"Nice Nebby, don't cry!" Kiawe comforted the Pokémon, before passing it to Mallow in a panic.

Mallow's Steenee began to twirl and whirl to try to calm down the creature. It worked! Nebby even began to giggle again.

"Phew!" sighed Professor Kukui. "Now that it's calm, let's find out what it likes to eat."

Ash and his friends took turns to offer the Pokémon a treat.

"Nebby? Do any of these things look yummy to you?" Ash asked it.

But the floating Pokémon refused everything it was offered – sandwiches, salad, even cake!

Sophocles had an idea. "Maybe this will work?" he smiled, holding up a bag of star candy.

Sweets shaped like stars were the perfect treat for the Pokémon! At last, it gobbled up the food.

"Looks like we're going to need to stock up on star candy!" Professor Kukui smiled.

Later that day, some visitors arrived at the Pokémon School. One of them was Lillie's mother, Lusamine, who was also president of the Aether Foundation. The Foundation was set up to protect and rescue Pokémon in trouble.

Lillie was surprised to see her. "Mother?" she gasped.

"My Lillie!" her mother smiled. "How's my baby?"

"I'm not a baby, please don't embarrass me!" Lillie replied crossly.

Lusamine introduced her team of researchers, Professor Burnet, Wicke and Faba.

"Without them, the foundation couldn't do its work!" Lusamine explained. "Now this may be rushed, but please could someone introduce us to Nebby?"

That was the reason they were here!

Ash showed the mysterious Pokémon to Lillie's mum, who tickled the creature gently.

"So precious!" Lusamine smiled.

Professor Burnet inspected Nebby next. "As I thought," said the scientist. "It seems to be an **Ultra Beast**."

"An Ultra Beast?" said Ash.

"A long, long time ago, some strange creatures from another world appeared and challenged the Island Guardians to a terrible battle," Professor Burnet explained. "Have you heard that legend before?"

"You really think that Nebby is one of these 'Ultra Beasts'?" Ash asked, shocked.

"Any physical thing with some connection to that other world, as well as the Ultra Beasts themselves, emit a kind of aura. Our lab constantly measures it," said Professor Burnet.

"Last night we measured an enormous spike in the aura's power, near the Altar of the Sunne on Poni Island," Wicke added.

"That's the place!" gasped Ash.

Now everyone was puzzled!

"What's the place?" asked Rotom.

"That's where I was in my dream. And there were two really cool-looking Pokémon that appeared from the sky, Solgaleo and Lunala. And right after that, Nebby appeared from a blinding light …"

No one spoke for a second, as they tried to make sense of what Ash had just told them.

"Solgaleo? Lunala? We only know those names through legends. And now they've both appeared to you!" Lusamine pondered. It was obvious she believed him.

"It's just a child's dream!" scoffed Faba.

"Ash, you must allow the Aether Foundation to look after Nebby," Lusamine said, approaching him. "The Foundation gives every Pokémon the respect, love and care it needs. It will be in good hands!"

Ash shook his head. "I made a promise! I promised Solgaleo and Lunala that I'd take good care of Nebby. So I'll be looking after it myself!"

Faba was much less patient. "Young man, Ultra Beasts are far too much of a burden for a child like yourself to handle," he said firmly.

But Lillie stood up for her friend. "You should know that not only is Ash an extremely strong Trainer, but he also received a Z-Ring and Z-Crystal directly from Tapu Koko," she told the visitors.

"Tapu Koko? Melemele's Island Guardian? Wow!" said Wicke.

"Our Ash is quite the promising young Trainer!" Professor Kukui added. "He's already won grand trials on both Melemele and Akala islands."

"Ash can handle this," said Lusamine, impressed. She turned to Ash. "Solgaleo and Lunala entrusted this young Pokémon to your care."

"That's amazing!" Lillie gasped excitedly.

"Ash, if you run into any kind of trouble just contact me," Lusamine told the young Trainer, as the guests got ready to leave.

"Sure!" Ash nodded.

With that, Nebby yawned happily and closed its eyes.

"It's asleep again!" Ash laughed.

"We have enough problems with sleepyheads as it is!" Rotom joked.

What a day! What began with a strange dream saw Ash end the day with a brand-new friend! While he doesn't yet know whether Nebby is in fact an Ultra Beast, Ash has promised to take care of the creature himself. Perhaps when Nebby wakes up again Ash will get some answers!
Their Alola journey continues on page 50.

ALOLAN A-Z

As Ash and Pikachu continue their adventures in the Alola region, more exciting new Pokémon and rare Ultra Beasts are waiting to be discovered. Read on to meet some cool and surprising creatures!

ARAQUANID

Type:
Water – Bug

Height & weight:
1.8 m/82.0 kg

About: In battle, Araquanid uses the water bubble that surrounds its head as a weapon, headbutting its opponents or cutting off their air. When it's not battling, it uses the bubble as a shield to protect its weaker companions.

BEWEAR

Type:
Normal – Fighting

Height & weight:
2.1 m/135.0 kg

About: Think twice before making friends with a Bewear. This super-strong Pokémon might be even more dangerous to those it likes, because it tends to deliver bone-crushing hugs as a sign of affection. Beware!

BOUNSWEET

Type:
Grass

Height & weight:
0.3 m/3.2 kg

About: Bounsweet smells good enough to eat – which sometimes gets it into trouble! The intensely sugary liquid it gives off can be diluted to bring the sweetness level down so people can drink it.

BRIONNE

Type:
Water

Height & weight:
0.6 m/17.5 kg

About: Brionne pelts its opponents with water balloons in a swift and skilful battle dance. It also shows off its dancing abilities when trying to cheer up its Trainer.

BRUXISH

Type:
Water – Psychic

Height & weight:
0.9 m/19.0 kg

About: Don't let the beguiling grin of the brightly coloured Bruxish fool you – those teeth are strong and sharp, and it can wield psychic powers mighty enough to stun an opponent in battle.

BUZZWOLE

ULTRA BEAST

Type:
Bug – Fighting

Height & weight:
2.4 m/333.6 kg

About: Buzzwole, one of the mysterious Ultra Beasts, is enormously strong, capable of demolishing heavy machinery with a punch. When it displays its impressive muscles, no one is sure whether it's just showing off – or issuing a threat.

CELESTEELA

ULTRA BEAST

Type:
Steel – Flying

Height & weight:
9.2 m/999.9 kg

About: Celesteela, one of the mysterious Ultra Beasts, can shoot incendiary gases from its arms and has been known to burn down wide swathes of trees. In flight, it can reach impressive speeds.

CHARJABUG

Type:
Bug – Electric

Height & weight:
0.5 m/10.5 kg

About: When Charjabug breaks down food for energy, some of that energy is stored as electricity inside its body. A Trainer who likes to go camping would appreciate having this Pokémon as a partner!

COMFEY

Type:
Fairy

Height & weight:
0.1 m/0.3 kg

About: Comfey collects flowers and attaches them to its vine, where they flourish and release a calming fragrance. Adding these flowers to bathwater makes for a relaxing soak.

COSMOEM

Type:
Psychic

Height & weight:
0.1 m/999.9 kg

About: Cosmoem never moves, radiating a gentle warmth as it develops inside the hard shell that surrounds it. Long ago, people referred to it as the cocoon of the stars, and some still think its origins lie in another world.

COSMOG

Type:
Psychic

Height & weight:
0.2 m/0.1 kg

About: Cosmog reportedly came to the Alola region from another world, but its origins are shrouded in mystery. Known as the child of the stars, it grows by gathering dust from the atmosphere.

CRABOMINABLE

Type:
Fighting – Ice

Height & weight:
1.7 m/180.0 kg

About: Covered in warm fur, Crabominable evolved from Crabrawler that took their goal of aiming for the top a bit too literally and found themselves at the summit of icy mountains. They can detach their pincers and fling them at foes.

CRABRAWLER

Type:
Fighting

Height & weight:
0.6 m/7.0 kg

About: Crabrawler is always looking for a fight, and it really hates to lose. Sometimes its pincers come right off because it uses them for punching so much! Fortunately, it can regrow them quickly.

CUTIEFLY

Type:
Bug – Fairy

Height & weight:
0.1 m/0.2 kg

About: Cutiefly can sense the aura of flowers and gauge when they're ready to bloom, so it always knows where to find fresh nectar. If you notice a swarm of these Pokémon following you around, you might have a floral aura!

DARTRIX

Type:
Grass – Flying

Height & weight:
0.7 m/16.0 kg

About: Dartrix is very conscious of its appearance and spends a lot of time keeping its wings clean. It can throw sharp-edged feathers, known as blade quills, with great accuracy.

DECIDUEYE

Type:
Grass – Ghost

Height & weight:
1.6 m/36.6 kg

About: A natural marksman, Decidueye can shoot its arrow quills with astonishing precision, hitting a tiny target a hundred yards away. It tends to be calm and collected, but sometimes panics if it's caught off guard.

DEWPIDER

Type:
Water – Bug

Height & weight:
0.3 m/4.0 kg

About: Mostly aquatic, Dewpider brings a water-bubble 'helmet' along when it ventures onto the land to look for food. The bubble also lends extra power when it headbutts an opponent.

DHELMISE

Type:
Ghost – Grass

Height & weight:
3.9 m/210.0 kg

About: When Dhelmise swings its mighty anchor, even the biggest Pokémon have to watch out! It snags seaweed floating past on the waves and scavenges detritus from the seafloor to add to its body.

DIGLETT

ALOLA FORM

Type:
Ground – Steel

Height & weight:
0.2 m/1.0 kg

About: The metal hairs that sprout from the top of Diglett's head can be used to communicate or to sense its surroundings. It can extend just those hairs above ground to make sure everything is safe before emerging.

DRAMPA

Type:
Normal – Dragon

Height & weight:
3.0 m/185.0 kg

About: Even wild Drampa have a real soft spot for kids. Though they make their home far away in the mountains, they often come into town to visit and play with the local children.

DUGTRIO

ALOLA FORM

Type:
Ground – Steel

Height & weight:
0.7 m/66.6 kg

About: Although Dugtrio's golden hair is shiny and beautiful, people aren't inclined to collect it when it falls – there are stories that doing so will bring bad luck. In Alola, this Pokémon is thought to represent the spirit of the land.

EXEGGUTOR

ALOLA FORM

Type:
Grass – Dragon

Height & weight:
10.9 m/415.6 kg

About: In the tropical sun and sand, Exeggutor grows exceptionally tall, unlocking draconic powers hidden deep within. Trainers in Alola are proud of the tree-like Exeggutor and consider this to be its ideal form.

FOMANTIS

Type:
Grass

Height & weight:
0.3 m/1.5 kg

About: Fomantis sleeps the day away, basking in the sunlight. The sweet scent it gives off sometimes attracts Cutiefly to its hiding place. During the night, it seeks out a safe place to sleep for the next day.

GEODUDE

ALOLA FORM

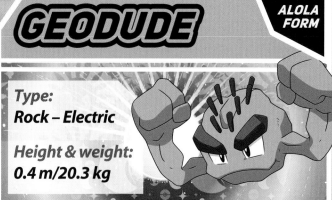

Type:
Rock – Electric

Height & weight:
0.4 m/20.3 kg

About: In the Alola region, Geodude are naturally magnetic, and their bodies are often covered in iron particles they've picked up while sleeping in the sand. Stepping on one can cause a nasty shock, so beachgoers keep a sharp eye out.

GOLEM

ALOLA FORM

Type:
Rock – Electric

Height & weight:
1.7 m/316.0 kg

About: The rocks Golem fires from its back carry a strong electrical charge, so even a glancing blow can deliver a powerful shock. Sometimes it grabs a Geodude to fire instead.

GOLISOPOD

Type:
Bug – Water

Height & weight:
2.0 m/108.0 kg

About: When Golisopod has to battle, its six sharp-clawed arms are certainly up to the task. Most of the time, though, it lives quietly in underwater caves, where it meditates and avoids conflict.

GRAVELER

ALOLA FORM

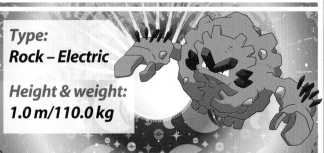

Type:
Rock – Electric

Height & weight:
1.0 m/110.0 kg

About: The crystals that appear on Graveler's body are the result of consuming dravite, a particularly tasty mineral. Graveler often fight over dravite deposits, crashing together with a sound like thunder.

GRIMER

ALOLA FORM

Type:
Poison – Dark

Height & weight:
0.7 m/42.0 kg

About: Grimer's appearance in the Alola region developed after it was called upon to deal with a persistent garbage problem. Each crystal on its body is formed from dangerous toxins, and those toxins escape if a crystal falls off.

GRUBBIN

Type:
Bug

Height & weight:
0.4 m/4.4 kg

About: Grubbin have discovered that sticking close to Electric-type Pokémon offers some protection from the Flying types that often like to attack them! With their strong jaws, they can scrape away tree bark to get at the delicious sap underneath.

GUMSHOOS

Type:
Normal

Height & weight:
0.7 m/14.2 kg

About: Gumshoos displays amazing patience when it's on a stakeout, waiting to ambush its prey. It's a natural enemy of Rattata, but the two rarely interact because they're awake at different times.

GUZZLORD

ULTRA BEAST

Type:
Dark – Dragon

Height & weight:
5.5 m/888.0 kg

About: Guzzlord, one of the mysterious Ultra Beasts, seems to have an insatiable appetite for just about everything – it will even swallow buildings and mountains. This constant munching can be very destructive.

HAKAMO-O

Type:
Dragon – Fighting

Height & weight:
1.2 m/47.0 kg

About: Hakamo-o regularly sheds its scales and grows new ones. Each set of scales is harder and sharper than the one before. It leaps at opponents with a battle cry, and the sharp scales turn its punches into a real threat.

INCINEROAR

Type:
Fire – Dark

Height & weight:
1.8 m/83.0 kg

About: Training an Incineroar requires patience – if it's not in just the right mood, it shows complete disregard for any orders given. During battle, it throws fierce punches and kicks, then launches the flames on its belly in a final attack.

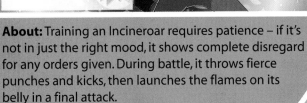

JANGMO-O

Type:
Dragon

Height & weight:
0.6 m/29.7 kg

About: Wild Jangmo-o live in remote mountains, far away from people. When they smack their scales together, either in battle or to communicate, the mountains ring with the metallic sound.

KARTANA

Type:
Grass – Steel

Height & weight:
0.3 m/0.1 kg

About: Kartana, one of the mysterious Ultra Beasts, can use its entire sharp-edged body as a weapon in battle. Its blade is strong and sharp enough to slice right through a steel structure in a single stroke.

KOMALA

Type:
Normal

Height & weight:
0.4 m/19.9 kg

About: Komala never wakes up – ever – although it does sometimes move around as it dreams. It lives in a permanent state of sleep, cuddling its precious log or its Trainer's arm.

KOMMO-O

Type:
Dragon – Fighting

Height & weight:
1.6 m/78.2 kg

About: Long ago, Kommo-o scales were collected for use in battle. For this Pokémon, the scales provide offence, defence, and even a warning system – when it shakes its tail, the scales clash together in a jangle that scares off weak opponents.

LITTEN

Type:
Fire

Height & weight:
0.4 m/4.3 kg

About: When it grooms its fur, Litten stores up the fur in its stomach to later launch as fiery attacks. Trainers often have a hard time getting this solitary Pokémon to trust them.

LUNALA

Type:
Psychic – Ghost

Height & weight:
4.0 m/120.0 kg

About: Lunala's wide wings soak up the light, plunging the brightest day into shadow. This Legendary Pokémon apparently makes its home in another world, and it returns there when its third eye becomes active.

LURANTIS

Type:
Grass

Height & weight:
0.9 m/18.5 kg

About: It can be difficult to give Lurantis the proper care to keep its colouring bright and vivid, but some Trainers enthusiastically accept the challenge. The beams it shoots from its petals can pierce thick metal.

LYCANROC

Type:
Rock

Height & weight:
0.8 m/25.0 kg

About: Its thick mane conceals sharp rocks that it uses in battle along with its fangs and claws. Despite its fearsome arsenal, Lycanroc displays fierce loyalty toward a Trainer who has raised it well.

LYCANROC

Type:
Rock

Height & weight:
0.8 m/25.0 kg

About: Lycanroc's Dusk Form is a rare sight in Alola. It only appears when a Rockruff evolves at sunset, during the time between day and night. This Pokémon's calm demeanour hides a strong impulse to battle.

LYCANROC

Type:
Rock

Height & weight:
1.1 m/25.0 kg

About: When Lycanroc faces a truly intimidating opponent, it attacks recklessly, with no concern for its own hide. The rocks in its mane contribute to the crushing power of its headbutt.

MAGEARNA

Type:
Steel – Fairy

Height & weight:
1.0 m/80.5 kg

About: Magearna was built many centuries ago by human inventors. The rest of this Pokémon's mechanical body is just a vehicle for its true self: the Soul-Heart contained in its chest.

MAREANIE

Type:
Poison – Water

Height & weight:
0.4 m/8.0 kg

About: Mareanie lives at the bottom of the sea or along the beach. It attacks with its head spike, which delivers poison that can weaken a foe. It's often tempted by the brightly coloured coral of Corsola.

MAROWAK

Type:
Fire – Ghost

Height & weight:
1.0 m/34.0 kg

About: The flaming bone that Marowak spins like a baton once belonged to its mother, and it's protected by its mother's spirit. It grieves for its fallen companions, visiting their graves along the roadside.

MARSHADOW

Type:
Fighting – Ghost

Height & weight:
0.7 m/22.2 kg

About: Very few people have seen Marshadow, so it was considered a rumour. Always cowering in the shadows, it watches others closely and mimics their movements.

MEOWTH

ALOLA FORM

Type:
Dark

Height & weight:
0.4 m/4.2 kg

About: Meowth is very vain about the golden Charm on its forehead, becoming enraged if any dirt dulls its bright surface. These crafty Pokémon are not native to Alola, but thanks to human interference, their population has surged.

MIMIKYU

Type:
Ghost – Fairy

Height & weight:
0.2 m/0.7 kg

About: What does Mimikyu look like? No one really knows, but apparently it's terrifying – it always hides underneath an old rag so it doesn't scare anyone while it's trying to make friends.

MINIOR

METEOR FORM

Type:
Rock – Flying

Height & weight:
0.3 m/40.0 kg

About: Minior came into being when tiny particles in the ozone layer underwent mutation. When its shell becomes too heavy, it falls to the ground, and the impact can knock its shell clean off.

MINIOR

RED CORE

Type:
Rock – Flying

Height & weight:
0.3 m/0.3 kg

About: The atmospheric dust that Minior consumes influences the colour of its core. When the core is exposed, it's extremely vulnerable, and Trainers are advised to get it into a Poké Ball immediately for protection.

MORELULL

Type:
Grass – Fairy

Height & weight:
0.2 m/1.5 kg

About: The spores that Morelull gives off flicker with a hypnotic light that sends viewers to sleep. During the day, it plants itself beside a tree to absorb nutrients from the roots while it naps.

MUDBRAY

Type:
Ground

Height & weight:
1.0 m/110.0 kg

About: Mudbray just loves to get dirty, but it isn't just for fun. Playing in the mud actually gives it better traction for running – when its hooves are covered in dirt, they're less likely to slip, and it can run faster.

MUDSDALE

Type:
Ground

Height & weight:
2.5 m/920.0 kg

About: With the help of the mud that coats its hooves, Mudsdale can deliver heavy kicks powerful enough to demolish a big truck. The mud it produces is weather-resistant, and people used to use it to shore up their houses.

MUK
ALOLA FORM

Type:
Poison – Dark

Height & weight:
1.0 m/52.0 kg

About: Muk's bright and colourful markings are the result of chemical changes in its body, caused by its diet of all sorts of garbage. It's generally a pleasant and friendly companion, but if it gets hungry, it can turn destructive.

NECROZMA

Type:
Psychic

Height & weight:
2.4 m/230.0 kg

About: Some think Necrozma arrived from another world many eons ago. When it emerges from its underground slumber, it seems to absorb light for use as energy to power its laser-like blasts.

NIHILEGO
ULTRA BEAST

Type:
Rock – Poison

Height & weight:
1.2 m/55.5 kg

About: Nihilego, one of the mysterious Ultra Beasts, can apparently infest other beings and incite them to violence. Research is inconclusive as to whether this Pokémon can think for itself, but it sometimes exhibits the behaviour of a young girl.

NINETALES
ALOLA FORM

Type:
Ice – Fairy

Height & weight:
1.1 m/19.9 kg

About: In its frosty coat, Ninetales creates ice droplets that can be used to shower over opponents. It's generally calm and collected, but if it becomes angry, it can freeze the offenders in their tracks.

ORANGURU

Type:
Normal – Psychic

Height & weight:
1.5 m/76.0 kg

About: Extremely intelligent and somewhat particular, Oranguru can be a bad fit for Trainers who lack experience. In the wild, it spends most of its time in the jungle canopy, though it sometimes emerges in search of an intellectual challenge.

ORICORIO

BAILE STYLE

Type:
Fire – Flying

Height & weight:
0.6 m/3.4 kg

About: Drinking red nectar gives Oricorio a fiery style when it dances. It's best to enjoy this beautiful performance from a distance, because its beating wings give off scorching flames.

ORICORIO

PA'U STYLE

Type:
Psychic – Flying

Height & weight:
0.6 m/3.4 kg

About: Drinking pink nectar transforms Oricorio into a hypnotically swaying dancer. As its opponents watch, entranced, the swaying movement relaxes Oricorio's mind so it can build up psychic energy for attacks.

ORICORIO

POM-POM STYLE

Type:
Electric – Flying

Height & weight:
0.6 m/3.4 kg

About: Drinking yellow nectar makes Oricorio's dance style truly electric. The charge generated by the rubbing of its feathers allows it to land shocking punches in battle as it performs a cheerful dance.

ORICORIO

SENSU STYLE

Type:
Ghost – Flying

Height & weight:
0.6 m/3.4 kg

About: Drinking purple nectar inspires Oricorio to perform a dreamy and elegant dance. The spirits of the departed are drawn to this beautiful performance, and Oricorio channels their power into its attacks.

PALOSSAND

Type:
Ghost – Ground

Height & weight:
1.3 m/250.0 kg

About: In order to evolve, this Pokémon took control of people playing in the sand to build up its body into a sand castle. Those who disappear can sometimes be found buried underneath Palossand, drained of their vitality.

PASSIMIAN

Type:
Fighting

Height & weight:
2.0 m/82.8 kg

About: Passimian are real team players – they learn from each other and work together for the benefit of the group. Each group, composed of about 20 Passimian, shares a remarkably strong bond.

PERSIAN

Type:
Dark

Height & weight:
1.1 m/33.0 kg

About: Trainers in Alola adore Persian for its coat, which is very smooth and has a velvety texture. This Pokémon has developed a haughty attitude and prefers to fight dirty when it gets into battle.

PHEROMOSA

ULTRA BEAST

Type:
Bug – Fighting

Height & weight:
1.8 m/25.0 kg

About: Pheromosa, one of the mysterious Ultra Beasts, seems to be extremely wary of germs and won't touch anything willingly. Witnesses have seen it charging through the region at amazing speeds.

PIKIPEK

Type:
Normal – Flying

Height & weight:
0.3 m/1.2 kg

About: Pikipek can drill into the side of a tree at the rate of 16 pecks per second! It uses the resulting hole as a place to nest and to store berries – both for food and for use as projectiles.

POPPLIO

Type:
Water

Height & weight:
0.4 m/7.5 kg

About: Popplio uses the water balloons it blows from its nose in battle. It's a hard worker and puts in lots of practice creating and controlling these balloons.

PRIMARINA

Type:
Water – Fairy

Height & weight:
1.8 m/44.0 kg

About: This Pokémon's singing voice is a delicate and powerful tool, used to attack its foes and to control the water balloons it creates. Groups of Primarina teach these battle songs to the next generation.

PYUKUMUKU

Type:
Water

Height & weight:
0.3m/1.2 kg

About: Pyukumuku has a remarkable and revolting tactic in battle: it can spew out its innards to strike at its opponent. It's covered in a sticky slime that beachgoers use to soothe their skin after a sunburn.

RAICHU

Type:
Electric – Psychic

Height & weight:
0.7 m/21.0 kg

About: Researchers speculate that Raichu looks different in the Alola region because of what it eats. It can 'surf' on its own tail, standing on the flat surface and using psychic power to raise itself off the ground.

RATICATE

Type:
Dark – Normal

Height & weight:
0.7 m/25.5 kg

About: Each Raticate leads a group of Rattata, and the groups regularly scuffle over food. This Pokémon is rather picky about what it eats, so a restaurant where a Raticate lives is likely to be a good one.

RATTATA

Type:
Dark – Normal

Height & weight:
0.3 m/3.8 kg

About: Rattata sleep during the day and spend their nights searching for the best food to bring back to the Raticate who leads them. They use their strong teeth to gnaw their way into people's kitchens.

RIBOMBEE

Type:
Bug – Fairy

Height & weight:
0.2 m/0.5 kg

About: Ribombee gathers up pollen and forms it into a variety of puffs with different effects. Some enhance battle skills and can be used as supplements, while others deliver excellent nutrition.

ROCKRUFF

Type:
Rock

Height & weight:
0.5 m/9.2 kg

About: Rockruff has a long history of living in harmony with people. This friendly Pokémon is often recommended for Trainers just starting their journey, although it tends to develop a bit of a wild side as it grows.

ROWLET

Type:
Grass – Flying

Height & weight:
0.3 m/1.5 kg

About: During the day, Rowlet rests and generates energy via photosynthesis. In the night, it flies silently to sneak up on foes and launch a flurry of kicking attacks.

SALANDIT

Type:
Poison – Fire

Height & weight:
0.6 m/4.8 kg

About: Salandit gives off a toxic gas that causes dizziness and confusion when inhaled. It uses this gas to distract opponents before attacking. These Pokémon can often be found living on the slopes of volcanoes.

SALAZZLE

Type:
Poison – Fire

Height & weight:
1.2 m/22.2 kg

About: Apparently, all Salazzle are female. They tend to attract several male Salandit and live together in a group. The poisonous gas they give off contains powerful pheromones and is sometimes used as a perfume ingredient.

SANDSHREW ALOLA FORM

Type:
Ice – Steel

Height & weight:
0.7 m/40.0 kg

About: Sandshrew lives high in the snowy mountains of Alola, where it has developed a shell of thick steel. It's very good at sliding across the ice – whether it does so under its own power or as part of a Sandshrew-sliding contest!

SANDSLASH ALOLA FORM

Type:
Ice – Steel

Height & weight:
1.2 m/55.0 kg

About: Sandslash is covered in spikes of tough steel, and in the cold mountains where it lives, each spike develops a thick coating of ice. A plume of snow flies up behind it as it dashes across the snowfield.

SANDYGAST

Type:
Ghost – Ground

Height & weight:
0.5 m/70.0 kg

About: A child created a mound of sand while playing on the beach, and it became a Sandygast. Putting your hand in its mouth is a sure way to fall prey to its mind control.

SHIINOTIC

Type:
Grass – Fairy

Height & weight:
1.0 m/11.5 kg

About: It's a bad idea to wander in Shiinotic's forest home at night. The strange, flickering lights given off by this Pokémon's spores can confuse travellers and cause them to lose their way.

SILVALLY

Type:
Normal

Height & weight:
2.3 m/100.5 kg

About: Learning to trust its Trainer caused this Pokémon to evolve and discard the mask that kept its power tightly controlled. Silvally can change its type in battle, making it a formidable opponent.

SOLGALEO

Type:
Pyschic – Steel

Height & weight:
3.4 m/230.0 kg

About: Solgaleo's entire body radiates a bright light that can wipe away the darkness of night. This Legendary Pokémon apparently makes its home in another world, and it returns there when its third eye becomes active.

STEENEE

Type:
Grass

Height & weight:
0.7 m/8.2 kg

About: Lively and cheerful, Steenee often attracts a crowd of other Pokémon drawn to its energy and its lovely scent. Its sepals have evolved into a hard shell to protect its head and body from attackers.

STUFFUL

Type:
Normal – Fighting

Height & weight:
0.5 m/6.8 kg

About: Petting an unfamiliar Stufful is a bad idea, even though it's really cute – it dislikes being touched by anyone it doesn't consider a friend, and responds with a flailing of limbs that can knock over a strong fighter.

TAPU BULU

Type:
Grass – Fairy

Height & weight:
1.9 m/45.5 kg

About: Tapu Bulu has a reputation for laziness – rather than battling directly, it commands vines to pin down its foes. The plants that grow abundantly in its wake give it energy. It's known as the guardian of Ula'ula Island.

TAPU FINI

Type:
Water – Fairy

Height & weight:
1.3 m/21.2 kg

About: Tapu Fini can control and cleanse water, washing away impurities. When threatened, it summons a dense fog to confuse its enemies. This Pokémon draws energy from ocean currents. It's known as the guardian of Poni Island.

TAPU KOKO

Type:
Electric – Fairy

Height & weight:
1.8 m/20.5 kg

About: Somewhat lacking in attention span, Tapu Koko is quick to anger but just as quickly forgets why it's angry. Calling thunderclouds lets it store up lightning as energy. It's known as the guardian of Melemele Island.

TAPU LELE

Type:
Psychic – Fairy

Height & weight:
1.2 m/18.6 kg

About: As Tapu Lele flutters through the air, people in search of good health gather up the glowing scales that fall from its body. It draws energy from the scent of flowers. It's known as the guardian of Akala Island.

TOGEDEMARU

Type:
Electric – Steel

Height & weight:
0.3 m/3.3 kg

About: Its back is covered with long, spiny fur that usually lies flat. Togedemaru can bristle up the fur during battle for use as a weapon, or during storms to attract lightning, which it stores as electricity in its body.

TORRACAT

Type:
Fire

Height & weight:
0.7 m/25.0 kg

About: Torracat attacks with powerful punches from its front legs, which are strong enough to bend iron. When it spits flames, the fiery bell at its throat starts to ring.

TOUCANNON

Type:
Normal – Flying

Height & weight:
1.1 m/26.0 kg

About: The inside of Toucannon's beak gets very hot during a battle – over 90 degrees Celsius. The heat fuels its explosive seed-shooting and can also give opponents a serious scorching!

TOXAPEX

Type:
Poison – Water

Height & weight:
0.7 m/14.5 kg

About: It's a good thing Toxapex lives at the bottom of the ocean, because its poison is very dangerous. Those who fall prey to it can expect three very painful days before they recover, and the effects can linger.

TRUMBEAK

Type:
Normal – Flying

Height & weight:
0.6 m/14.8 kg

About: Trumbeak stores berry seeds in its beak to use as projectiles. It attacks opponents with a rapid-fire burst of seeds. Its beak is also very good at making lots of noise!

TSAREENA

Type:
Grass

Height & weight:
1.2 m/21.4 kg

About: Beauty salons sometimes use images of the lovely Tsareena in their advertising. It can be a fierce fighter, using its long legs to deliver skilful kicks as it mocks its defeated opponent.

TURTONATOR

Type:
Fire – Dragon

Height & weight:
2.0 m/212.0 kg

About: Poisonous gases and flames spew from Turtonator's nostrils. Its shell is made of unstable material that might explode upon impact, so opponents are advised to aim for its stomach instead.

TYPE: NULL

Type:
Normal

Height & weight:
1.9 m/120.5 kg

About: The synthetic Pokémon known as Type: Null wears a heavy mask to keep its power in check. Some fear that without the mask, it would lose control of its powers and go on a destructive rampage.

VIKAVOLT

Type:
Bug – Electric

Height & weight:
1.5 m/45.0 kg

About: Vikavolt uses its large jaws to focus the electricity it produces inside its body, then unleashes a powerful zap to stun its opponents. Flying-type Pokémon that once posed a threat are no match for its shocking attacks.

VULPIX

Type:
Ice

Height & weight:
0.6 m/9.9 kg

About: Vulpix in the Alola region were once known as Keokeo, and some older folks still use that name. Its six tails can create a spray of ice crystals to cool itself off when it gets too hot.

WIMPOD

Type:
Bug – Water

Height & weight:
0.5 m/12.0 kg

About: When the cowardly Wimpod flees from battle, it leaves a path swept clean by the passing of its many legs. It helps keep the beaches and seabeds clean, too, scavenging just about anything edible.

WISHIWASHI

Type:
Water

Height & weight:
0.2 m/0.3 kg

About: If a Wishiwashi looks like it's about to cry, watch out! The light that shines from its watering eyes draws the entire school, and they band together to fight off their opponent by sheer strength of numbers.

WISHIWASHI

Type:
Water

Height & weight:
8.2 m/78.6 kg

About: On its own, Wishiwashi is a feeble opponent, but when many Wishiwashi come together in a school, they are known as the demon of the sea. Their combined power is enough to scare away a Gyarados.

XURKITREE

Type:
Electric

Height & weight:
3.8 m/100.0 kg

About: Xurkitree, one of the mysterious Ultra Beasts, invaded an electric plant after it emerged from the Ultra Wormhole. Some suspect it absorbs electricity into its body to power the serious shocks it gives off.

YUNGOOS

Type:
Normal

Height & weight:
0.4 m/6.0 kg

About: Yungoos is always on the move during the day, looking for food – and it's not too picky about what it bites with its sharp teeth. When night comes, it immediately falls asleep no matter where it happens to be.

FUNNY FEELINGS

Read the sentences, then draw lines to choose a face to show how Pikachu is feeling each time.

A

1

Pikachu meets an amazing Alolan Exeggutor for the first time.

B

2

Pikachu is ready for bed after training hard all day.

C

3

Ash gives Pikachu some delicious star candy.

4

Team Rocket tease Pikachu for being small.

D

THE ANSWERS ARE ON PAGE 69.

UNDERSEA ADVENTURE

Here's how to travel under the sea – in Popplio's perfect water balloon! Choose someone to draw inside – another Pokémon, Lana or even yourself!

SUN OR MOON ?

Cover up the right-hand page, then colour in the sun or moon symbols to show whether you think these Pokémon are active during the day or whether they come alive at night.

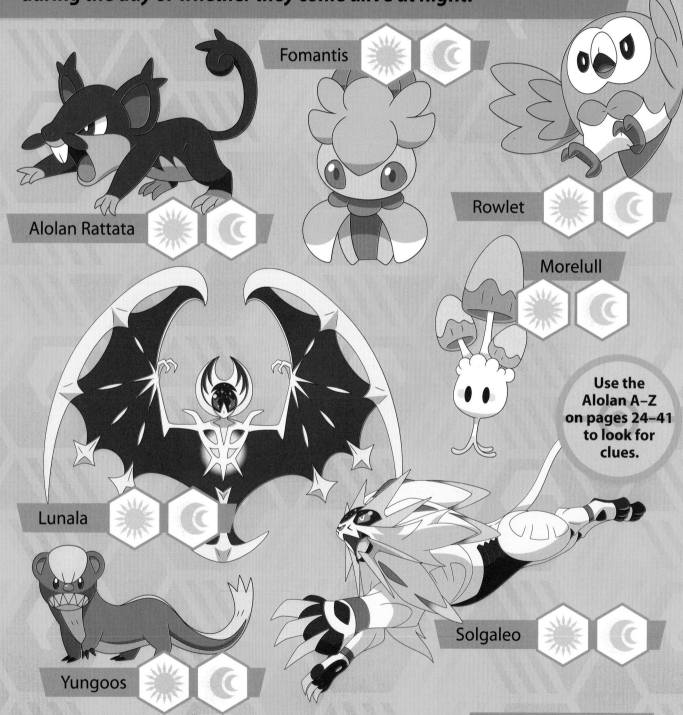

Fomantis

Alolan Rattata

Rowlet

Morelull

Lunala

Use the Alolan A–Z on pages 24–41 to look for clues.

Yungoos

Solgaleo

MY SCORE:

Now uncover the next page and read the descriptions to see how many you got right.

ALOLAN RATTATA

Rattata in their Alolan form spend their days fast asleep and their nights foraging for food to offer to their Raticate leader.

FOMANTIS

Fomantis soaks up sunlight all day while fast asleep. After dusk it awakes to search for a new spot to sleep the next day.

ROWLET

Rowlet's days are spent resting, while it generates energy from sunlight. Night time is when it comes alive – its opponents should beware!

LUNALA

Nocturnal Lunala's enormous wings soak up sunlight, turning daytime into the blackest of nights.

MORELULL

Morelull naps the whole day through while it takes in nutrients from the soil. Its energy is saved for night-time activity.

YUNGOOS

Yungoos's daytime search for food never ends. It's no wonder it falls asleep as soon as dusk falls!

SOLGALEO

Solgaleo's whole body glows with a light so powerful that the darkest of nights becomes a bright new day.

HOW TO DRAW ROWLET

Ash used Rowlet in his first island challenge trial in Alola. They've been good buddies ever since.

Follow the steps to draw this Grass-Flying-type Pokémon.

 Draw an egg shape, almost a circle. Sketch a faint cross, slightly to the left, as shown. You can rub this out later. Next, draw two rough shapes for Rowlet's feet.

2 Now draw a long oval shape for the beak and two smaller ovals for eyes, either side.

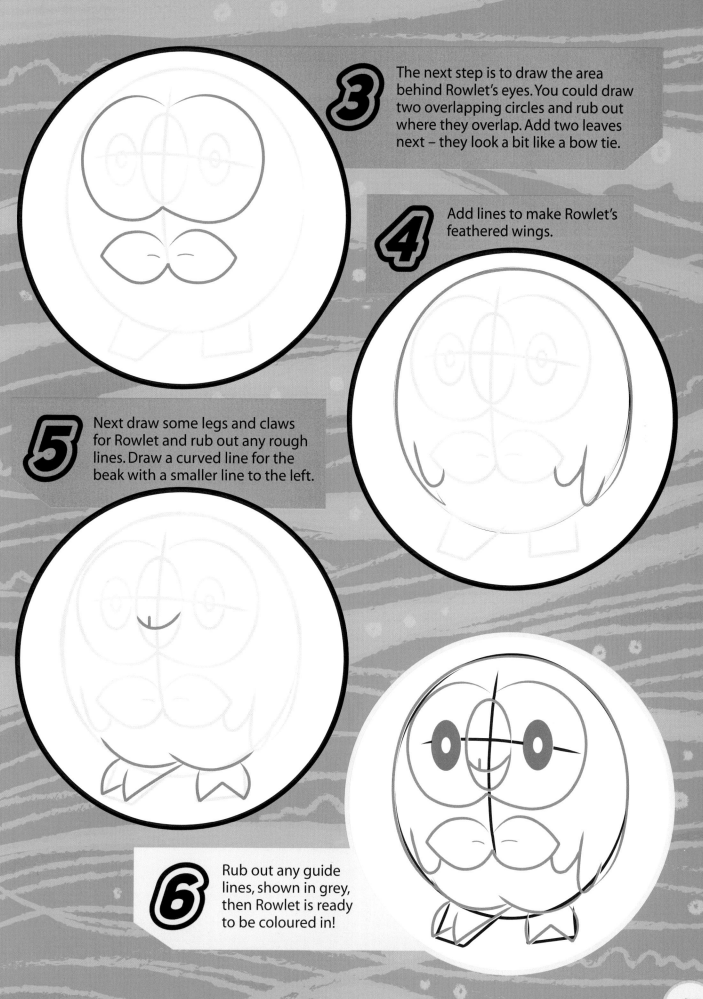

3 The next step is to draw the area behind Rowlet's eyes. You could draw two overlapping circles and rub out where they overlap. Add two leaves next – they look a bit like a bow tie.

4 Add lines to make Rowlet's feathered wings.

5 Next draw some legs and claws for Rowlet and rub out any rough lines. Draw a curved line for the beak with a smaller line to the left.

6 Rub out any guide lines, shown in grey, then Rowlet is ready to be coloured in!

ISLAND CHALLENGE

Akala Island was the second island that Ash and Pikachu visited to learn about new Pokémon. Can you spot 10 differences between these pictures?

THE ANSWERS ARE ON PAGE 69.

ROCKY ROUTE

Help Ash and Pikachu make their way safely back to the city. Watch out for Alolan Geodudes – these Pokémon are highly charged!

THE ANSWERS ARE ON PAGE 69.

START

FINISH

Fact! Ash first discovered the Rock-Electric-type Alolan Geodude on Akala Island.

NOW YOU SEE THEM, NOW YOU DON'T!

With another day at the Pokémon School ahead, Ash was up early. He couldn't wait to get to school to find out more about the curious Pokémon in his care. Would today be the day that he and his friends discovered that Nebby was actually an **Ultra Beast**?

Outside the school, Team Rocket had set up a snack bar to raise funds for their evil operations and were each wearing a brand-new disguise. The sweet scent of baking doughnuts had just got them their first customer.

"Something smells good!" smiled Ash, approaching the snack van.

"Pika! Pika!" Pikachu agreed.

Nebby floated out from Ash's backpack to take a look at the sweet treats, too.

But there wasn't time for a snack, Professor Kukui called to Ash to head into school.

"Did you see that?" gasped Jessie, when they had gone. "That Pokémon must be incredibly rare."

"Purple body? Check. Gaseous features? Check. **A rarer-than-rare Pokémon** … and I know what it is!" smirked James.

"Tell me!" begged Jessie.

"A Protokoffing!" said James.

Jessie scratched her head. She had never heard of such a Pokémon!

"Just as a Pikachu evolves from a Pichu, I'm certain *that* Pokémon is Koffing's pre-evolved form, Protokoffing!" James explained.

"Well, well," smiled Meowth. "When you say it with such confidence, I believe you!"

In class, the day's first lesson was about to begin.

"Today, you're going to be sculpting a model of your Pokémon partner out of clay," Professor Kukui announced. "Closely observing your Pokémon while you work might lead you to discover something about them."

"Who should I make?" Ash pondered. "Nebby and Rowlet are asleep … Pikachu, I choose you!"

Lana began to sculpt Popplio, her Water-type Pokémon, while Lillie crafted a perfect Alolan Vulpix. But Ash's modelling was not going so well.

"Hmm, it looks more like a Mimikyu than a Pikachu," Professor Kukui smiled.

Sophocles was working on a clay Togedemaru.

Just then, Nebby woke up. It floated out of Ash's backpack, under Sophocles' desk and tickled him! Suddenly, Sophocles disappeared from the room and found himself at home with Jigglypuff! Seconds later, he was back in class.

Next, something equally strange happened to Lana. A touch from Nebby and she was instantly transported to the ocean. She returned to the classroom, soaking wet!

Mallow found herself with the huge Pokémon, Oranguru, while Kiawe's experience was red-hot! Nebby disappeared in a flash, taking Kiawe with him, as the other students looked on in amazement.

When he reappeared seconds later, Kiawe's hair had burst into flames. "HOT!" he yelled.

"Quick, Popplio! **Bubble Beam**!" Lana commanded. Her Pokémon blew a water balloon to quickly put out the fire.

"What just happened?" cried Kiawe. "I almost fell into a volcano!"

"That was Teleport!" Rotom explained. "Teleport allows the user to instantly travel from one location to another," said the floating Pokédex.

Ash was impressed. "Woah! I didn't know you could do that, Kiawe!" he said.

"I can't!" Kiawe said, puzzled.

But Lillie guessed how it had happened. "I think Nebby might have done it," she said.

Everyone looked surprised.

"Where did Nebby go, anyway?" wondered Sophocles.

The Pokémon had disappeared again! But the very next moment, Nebby was back! It floated on to a desk and fell fast asleep.

Later, over lunch, Lillie was testing out a theory she'd had about Nebby.

"At the moment you were Teleported … did your thoughts have anything to do with where you ended up?" she asked her friends.

Lillie was on to something! Mallow had been thinking about Oranguru, Lana had been dreaming of the ocean – as always – and Sophocles had thought that his Togedemaru model looked more like a Jigglypuff!

"I was thinking about the volcano in Akala!" Kiawe said.

"Nebby must have been reading whatever was on your minds and then Teleported every one of you there," said Lillie.

"I think you might be right," Sophocles agreed.

"Nebby is still so little, maybe it's trying to find a place to call home?" Mallow added.

"I wish Nebby would take me somewhere," Ash said sadly.

When Ash picked up the Pokémon, it was his turn to Teleport! First they went to Jigglypuff, next, to the ocean and then they found themselves with Oranguru.

The classmates looked at each other in surprise.

"They just disappeared!" exclaimed Rotom.

They waited and waited, but Ash and Pikachu didn't return.

"Let's go and look for them," Professor Kukui said.

Next, Lycanroc and Litten had the surprise of their lives!

"Phew! We're back home," sighed Ash, relieved to have landed in a safe place. Teleporting was terrifying, he decided.

But suddenly, Ash and Pikachu were on the move again.

The next place they found themselves was on a deserted beach, where Team Rocket were plotting their next wicked move.

"Protokoffing needs to be caught," said Jessie. "Suggestions?"

"Stake out the Pokémon School?" said James. "Nah – too many pesky kids."

"If only the boy turned up on this beach. It would make Pokémon pilfering so much easier," Jessie sighed.

Team Rocket couldn't believe their luck when Ash and Pikachu appeared with Nebby the next moment! They huddled together and whispered their motto, in turn.

"A single flower of evil is unfurled! It's Jessie!"

"The master of darkness in a tragic world! It's James!"

"A glittering dark star always shines bright!" Meowth added.

"Team Rocket, let's fight!" said Jessie and James together.

Ash approached the villains with caution. "What are you doing here?" he said.

"We're here to help! That Protokoffing you're holding … we'll take it off your hands!" said James politely.

Ash was puzzled. "Protokoffing?"

James pointed to the Pokémon in Ash's arms – Nebby!

"You've got to be kidding!" Ash replied.

There was only one way to resolve things – **a Pokémon Battle**.

"Let's fight fair and square," James pretended. He had a plan up his sleeve.

"We'll be keeping an eye out for dirty tricks!" smirked Meowth.

Jessie began with her Mimikyu. "Make those lame losers see stars!" she cackled.

"Be careful, Pikachu! Mimikyu's powerful!" Ash warned his buddy. He held on to Nebby tightly.

When the moment to attack came, Ash called. "Now, Pikachu, use **Electro Ball**!"

Pikachu hurled a glowing ball of electricity at Mimikyu, who easily dodged it. Ash paused to think about his next attack.

"Run out of moves already?" Jessie teased.

As Ash and Pikachu crept forwards, Mimikyu moved too, until the sun was directly behind it.

With Ash and Pikachu blinded by the sun's rays, Meowth saw its chance and made a grab for Nebby.

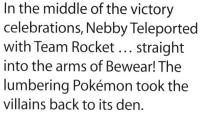

"You lose!" cheered Jessie. "Protokoffing's got a new family!"

"Hey! What happened to a fair and square fight?" Ash protested.

"Once a fool, always a fool!" James teased.

But it was Nebby who had the last laugh.

In the middle of the victory celebrations, Nebby Teleported with Team Rocket … straight into the arms of Bewear! The lumbering Pokémon took the villains back to its den.

Alone in the dark forest, Nebby began to feel scared. Then it knew where to go – home.

"Nebby!" gasped Ash. "I was worried you wouldn't come back!"

The Pokémon snuggled down in Ash's arms and closed its eyes.

"I know," Ash smiled, stroking the Pokémon. "You've had quite a day."

Suddenly …

"There they are!" called a voice. It was Kiawe and the others. "Where have you been?" he demanded.

"Shh!" Lillie said. "Nebby's sleeping."

"It used Teleport … a lot!" Ash explained. He began to tell them about all the places they had visited.

"Nebby's getting better at using Teleport," said Rotom. "I'm proud of it!"

"We'd better tell Professor Kukui," said Sophocles. "He's still out looking for Ash."

Ash looked sorry. He hadn't meant to cause his friends so much worry.

Nebby had one last Teleport to make with his new friends. In a flash, they were transported … to the rooftop of the Pokémon School!

"The classroom would have been better," laughed Kiawe. "Somebody **get us down**!"

It was another eventful day in Alola. When Nebby discovered how to Teleport, it took Ash and his friends on an adventure like never before! One thing is clear, Nebby is growing up and getting stronger. But the danger it faces is greater too – now Team Rocket knows about Nebby, the villains will stop at nothing to catch the rare Pokémon. What will happen next? Be sure to join Ash and his friends, as their Alolan journey continues!

CHANGING CREATURES

These awesome Alolan Pokémon evolve into even cooler creatures!
Follow the lines to discover the Evolutions.

Rockruff

Alolan Meowth

Stuful

Alolan Vulpix

Sandygast

THE
ANSWERS ARE
ON PAGE 69.

Bewear

Alolan
Ninetales

Palossand

Lycanroc
(Midday
Form)

Alolan
Persian

BEAUTIFUL BUGS

The Alola region is home to a host of Bug-type Pokémon and Ultra Beasts. Find their names in the word puzzle. The words read forwards, backwards, up, down and diagonally.

R	P	O	A	Q	U	A	R	A	Q	U	A	N	I	D
J	I	W	Q	R	T	L	S	H	X	K	G	F	X	J
U	F	B	Y	B	G	M	K	N	B	V	O	E	Q	N
D	C	U	O	C	R	W	C	J	U	F	L	Z	U	L
S	H	Z	J	M	U	V	U	D	Z	R	I	Y	D	F
R	P	G	S	V	B	F	T	C	Z	J	S	V	C	G
W	Q	X	E	R	B	E	I	B	W	M	O	H	P	U
H	D	F	D	P	I	J	E	R	O	D	P	X	K	B
V	O	S	W	Q	N	X	F	W	L	R	O	B	V	A
F	P	E	Y	D	U	R	L	U	E	K	D	J	Z	J
B	M	V	N	M	J	N	Y	Z	Y	D	Z	W	D	R
X	I	P	H	E	R	O	M	O	S	A	J	I	H	A
L	W	R	D	K	P	M	J	H	C	W	V	C	Z	H
I	D	K	C	W	Y	Q	Y	M	R	V	D	U	X	C
T	R	B	U	F	T	L	O	V	A	K	I	V	J	S

CHARJABUG **RIBOMBEE** **BUZZWOLE** **GOLISOPOD**
CUTIEFLY **VIKAVOLT** **PHEROMOSA**
GRUBBIN **WIMPOD** **ARAQUANID**

WHO'S THAT POKÉMON?
One little bug is feeling shy! Mix up all the shaded letters to work out who.

THE ANSWERS ARE ON PAGE 69.

STOP, THIEF!

Which hungry Pokémon is stealing berries from the fruit stand? Put the picture back in order to find out! The first one has been done for you.

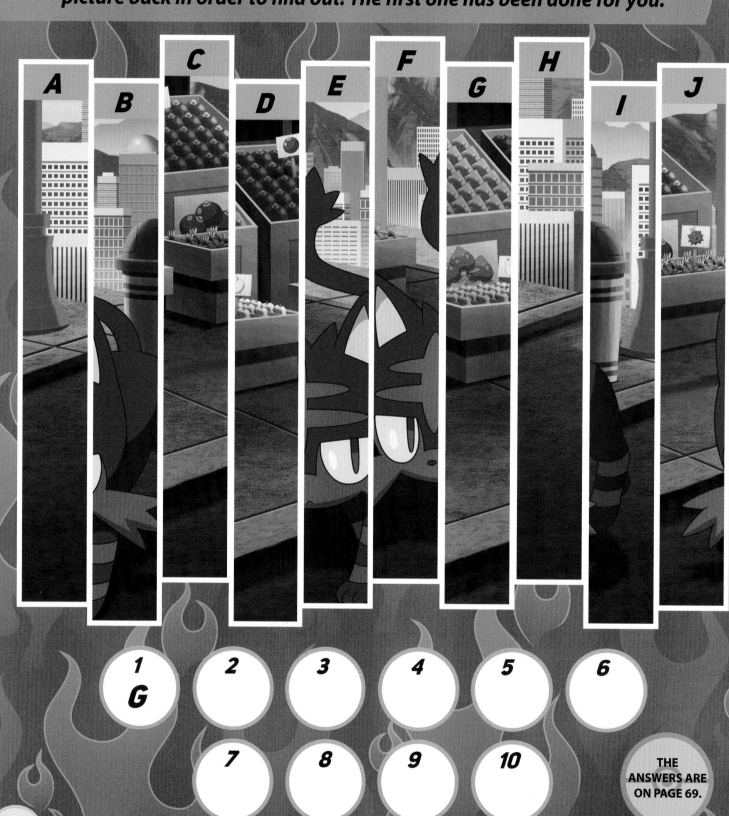

THE ANSWERS ARE ON PAGE 69.

MAKE A MASK

Look like Litten in this mega mask! Grab the things you'll need, then turn the page to see how to make your mask.

ASK AN ADULT TO HELP YOU MAKE THIS MASK.

You will need:

- scissors
- 1 piece of thin A4 card
- glue
- pencil
- string or elastic

Instructions

1 Carefully cut out the page, then keep these instructions safe.

2 Stick the rest of the page on to thin card.

3 Cut around the dotted lines of the mask, including the eye holes.

4 Cut 2 lengths of string or elastic and thread the string through the side holes.

5 Make a knot in one end of each piece to keep the string in place.

6 Finished! Try on your mask and tie the string tightly behind your head.

GUARDIANS OF ALOLA

How well do you know the island guardians of Alola? Draw lines to connect each guardian to its island name.

PONI

TAPU KOKO

TAPU FINI

AKALA

TAPU BULU

MELEMELE

TAPU LELE

ULA'ULA

THE ANSWERS ARE ON PAGE 69.

Now circle which Pokémon type each guardian is.

TAPU BULU

TAPU KOKO

TAPU FINI

TAPU LELE

 Electric Grass Psychic  Water Fairy

63

MAKING FACES

Litten and Popplio are just a couple of new faces that Ash has met in Alola. Take a look at these Pokémon patterns, then write or draw the missing Pokémon in each row.

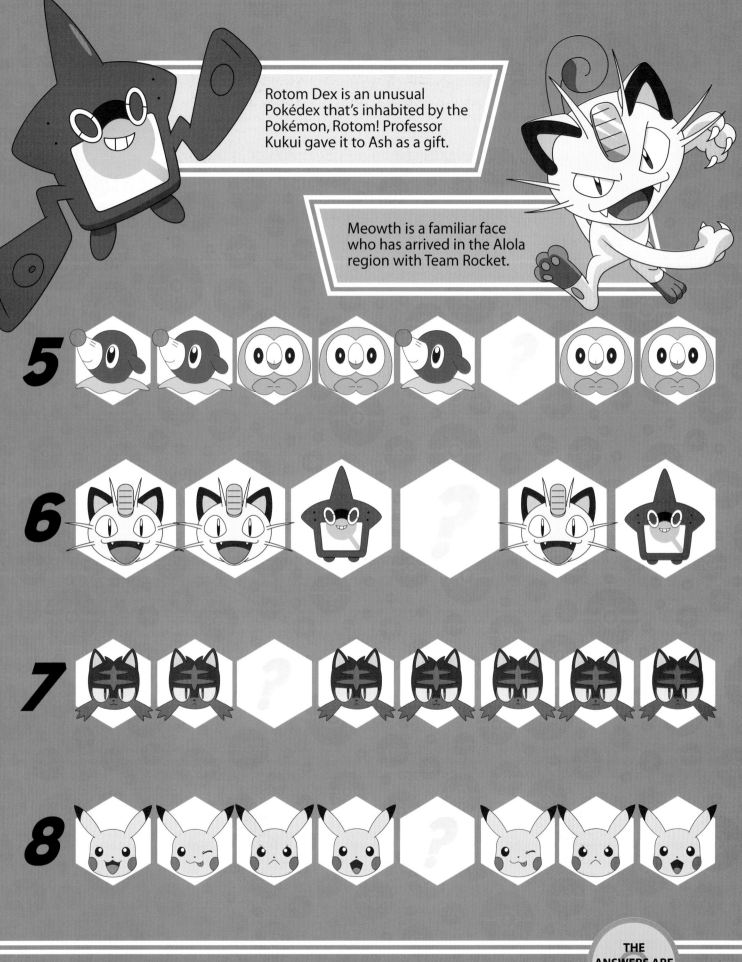

Rotom Dex is an unusual Pokédex that's inhabited by the Pokémon, Rotom! Professor Kukui gave it to Ash as a gift.

Meowth is a familiar face who has arrived in the Alola region with Team Rocket.

5

6

7

8

THE ANSWERS ARE ON PAGE 69.

FEARSOME FLYERS

**Draw lines to make pairs of formidable Flying-type Pokémon.
One Pokémon does not have a match – do you know why?**

THE ANSWERS ARE ON PAGE 69.

The odd one out is: _____ because _____

THAT HAT!

Can you guess which Pokémon has borrowed Ash's Alola hat? Join the dots to find out!

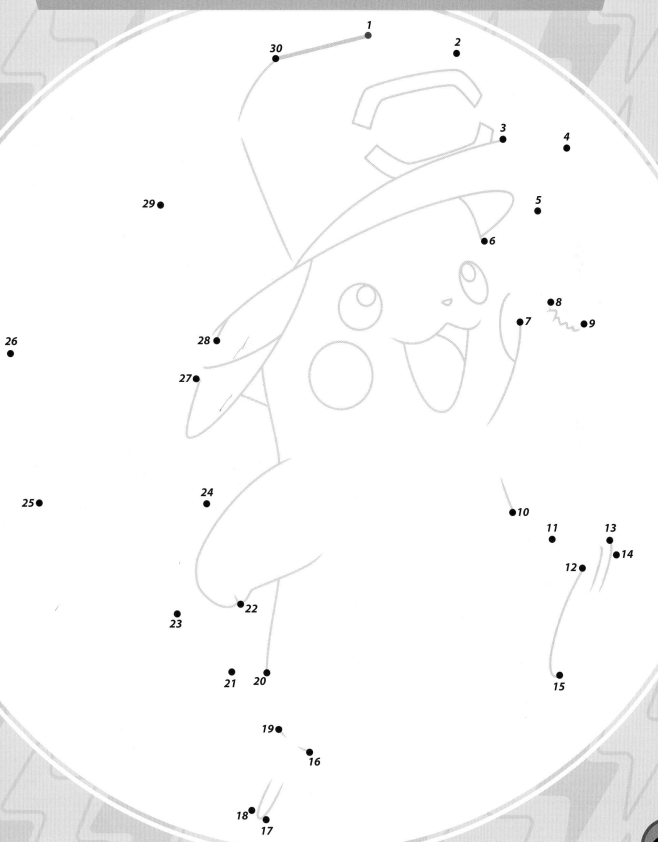

PIKACHU'S MOVES

Ash has trained Pikachu to use some cool moves in Pokémon battles. Read the descriptions, then fill in the missing letters to reveal which move Pikachu is unleashing.

1

Clue: A ball of electricity is blasted at the target in this mega move.

_LE_TR_ _ _LL

2

Clue: Pikachu uses his tail to deal his opponent a blow in this heavy-metal move.

I_ _N _ _ _L

3

Clue: Start running! No foe is safe when faced with this speedy offence.

_UI_ _ A_ _ _CK

4

Clue: Pikachu takes an enemy by storm! An electric move that will stop an opponent in its tracks.

_ _UN_ER_ _LT

THE ANSWERS ARE ON PAGE 69.

ANSWERS

PAGE 11

PAGE 14
Hit the Beach
The Pokémon is MAREANIE

PAGE 15 Sudoku

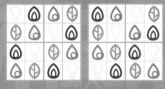

PAGE 42
Funny Feelings 1 – D, 2 – C, 3 – B, 4 – A.

PAGE 48 Island Challenge

PAGE 49
Rocky Route

PAGE 58 Changing Creatures
Rockruff – Lycanroc (Midday form)
Alolan Meowth – Alolan Persian
Stufful – Bewear
Alolan Vulpix – Alolan Ninetales
Sandygast – Palossand

PAGE 59 Beautiful Bugs

R	P	O	A	Q	U	A	R	A	Q	U	A	N	I	D
J	I	W	Q	R	T	L	S	H	X	K	G	F	X	J
U	F	B	Y	B	G	M	K	N	B	V	O	E	Q	N
D	C	U	O	C	R	W	C	J	U	F	L	Z	U	L
S	H	Z	J	M	U	V	U	D	Z	R	I	Y	D	F
R	P	G	S	V	B	F	T	C	Z	J	S	V	C	G
W	Q	X	E	R	B	E	I	B	W	M	O	H	P	U
H	D	F	D	P	I	J	E	R	O	D	P	X	K	B
V	O	S	W	Q	X	F	W	L	R	O	B	V	J	A
F	P	E	Y	D	U	R	L	U	E	K	D	J	Z	I
B	M	V	N	M	J	N	Y	Z	Y	D	Z	W	D	R
X	I	P	H	E	R	O	M	O	S	A	J	I	H	A
L	W	R	D	K	P	M	J	H	C	W	V	C	Z	H
I	D	K	C	W	Y	Q	M	R	V	D	U	X	C	S
T	R	B	U	F	T	L	O	V	A	K	I	V	J	S

Who's That Pokémon?
DEWPIDER

PAGE 60 Stop, Thief
1 – G, 2 – D, 3 – C, 4 – J, 5 – F, 6 – E,
7 – B, 8 – I, 9 – A, 10 – H.

PAGE 63 Guardians of Alola

PAGE 64 Making Faces

1
2
3
4
5
6
7
8

PAGE 66 Fearsome Flyers
A & E, B & F, C & H, D & I. The odd one out is
G. Cutiefly – it's not a Flying-type Pokémon.

PAGE 68 Pikachu's Moves
1 – ELECTRO BALL   2 – IRON TAIL
3 – QUICK ATTACK   4 – THUNDERBOLT